TELEVISION HATES ITSELF

by Phillip Barcio

illustrations by Mike Morelli

Published by Caprice Books
Santa Monica, CA, U.S.A.

For more information regarding this or any of
Caprice's other easy-to-carry books, email the
publisher at capricebooks@gmail.com.

Reply, if any, will be slow.

Insofar as this book expresses opinions, theories,
concepts, notions, thoughts or ideas, or inspires any
of the same, note that it is a work of the imagination.
Caprice Books and its contributors are not responsible
for any emotional, intellectual, psychological, or, such
as they might exist, spiritual conclusions arrived at by
the reader.

Printed on planet Earth.

"Television Hates Itself"
Second Edition
Written by Phillip Barcio
Illustrations by Mike Morelli
Published by Caprice Books, 2012
ISBN 978-0-9849159-2-7

Visit Caprice Books on the web:
capricebooks.blogspot.com

Do not expect much.

CAPRICE BOOKS

For Audrey.

TELEVISION HATES ITSELF

Television hates itself because it's predictable.

Television hates
itself because

it's a tool.

Television hates itself because it's obsessed with sports.

Television hates
itself because

it gets turned on for no
reason.

Television hates
itself because it's
obsessed with
being thin.

Television
hates itself because
it's old.

Television hates
itself because it
can't swim.

Television hates
itself because it's
manipulative.

Television hates
itself because no one in
their right mind would
want to marry it.

Television hates itself because it hasn't lived up to its potential.

Television hates
itself because
    it's under the
influence of
    prescription
drugs.

Television hates
itself because it

plays games.

Television hates
itself because it will
never be a real
girl.

Television hates
itself because it

can't get laid.

Television hates
itself because it's
American.

Television hates
itself because it

can't make a baby.

Television hates
itself because it
leads people on.

Television hates
itself for not being
more assertive.

Television hates
itself because it can
never hate you.

Television hates itself because of the way you've been looking at it lately.

Television hates
itself because it can't
    think of anything
else to do at the
    moment, except
laundry.

Television hates
itself because it
  shows how it's a
fool for your
  rodeo wild horses.

Television hates
itself because of what
it has done to
take our mood from
bad to worse.

Television hates
itself because it
needs you.

Television hates
itself because every
        mirror only shows
it what it can't be.

Television hates
itself because if it
had known you earlier it
would have been there.

Television hates
itself because it's a
stupid son of a
bitch who can't do
any damn thing
right.

Television hates itself because it wants to be happy like everyone else, but it was happy there, on that traffic island.

Television hates
itself because it
    knows on Monday
it's just going to
    be the same.

Television hates itself because of the hell it has put you through.

Television hates
itself because it's
    screwed up so
many times.

Television hates
itself because it can't
    stop this never-
ending battle to save
you all.

Television hates
itself because being
turned off causes it far
greater grief
than a million
people dying in a
Chinese earthquake.

Television hates
itself because of
its success.

Television hates
itself because it's
not satisfied.

Television hates itself because falsehood plays the biggest role in its conscious life.

Television hates itself because it's not attractive, but it's only into good-looking people.

Television hates
itself because it's
    just so much
easier that way.

Television hates
itself for spending so
much time talking
about celebrities'
baby daddies.

Television hates
itself because it
tries so hard to be
funny.

Television hates
itself because people
yell at it.

Television hates
itself because when
        it likes someone it
can never tell them.

Television hates
itself because it
                    never
wanted all this
influence.

Television hates
itself because it tries
to cram too much
into each day.

Television hates
itself because it

misrepresented
the meaning of
friendship.

Television hates
itself because it
doesn't have its
own apartment.

Television hates
itself because it

understands
everything it puts you
through.

Television hates
itself because you
    told it that it was
worthless and stupid
    and it kept
dwelling on it and it
turned to self-hate.

Television hates
itself because you

fight its advances,
even though you

seem to enjoy
them.

Television hates
itself because it's
square.

Television hates
itself because it's

clingy.

Television hates
itself for so often
saying it hates
itself, because it's
the most cliché
and stupid thing to say
over and over.

Television hates
itself because when it
sees him laid in the
manger,

in the lap of his
mother, and hears

the Angels sing, its
heart does not leap
into flame.

Television hates
itself because
          people make fun of
it.

Television hates itself because it can't leave.

Television hates
itself because of you.

Thanks.

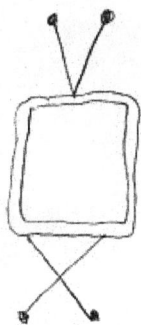

Television Hates Itself
was first presented in 2008 as a PowerPoint,
at Side Car Gallery in Indianapolis. Thirteen
handmade copies of the book were sold at
the show…or, more accurately, given away.

Phillip Barcio was born in Indiana, which means "Land of Indians" evidently in memory of the territory's earliest victims of aggravated robbery. He currently lives in California with his wife Audrey and their best friend, Elijah H. Huckleberry (the H. stands for Huckleberry). Here is a picture of Phillip from 1990:

Jazz musician and illustrator **Mike Morelli** created the beloved cartoon character Bobbo who appears in *Caprice Reader #1: If it won't reach...stretch*. Mike happened in Vegas sometime last century, but did not stay in Vegas. He currently lives in San Francisco with someone you should meet named Barbara. Here's a picture of Mike from 1980 inexplicably standing behind Jello Biafra:

Also Available from
CAPRICE BOOKS

Caprice Reader #1: "If it won't
reach...stretch."

and
Coming Soon from
CAPRICE BOOKS

Caprice Reader #2: "Powerless Point"

Buy Caprice Books at select establishments
throughout the physical world or on the
international webbie at
capricebooks.blogspot.com

www.ingramcontent.com/pod-product-compliance
Lightning Source LLC
Chambersburg PA
CBHW060424050426
42449CB00009B/2130